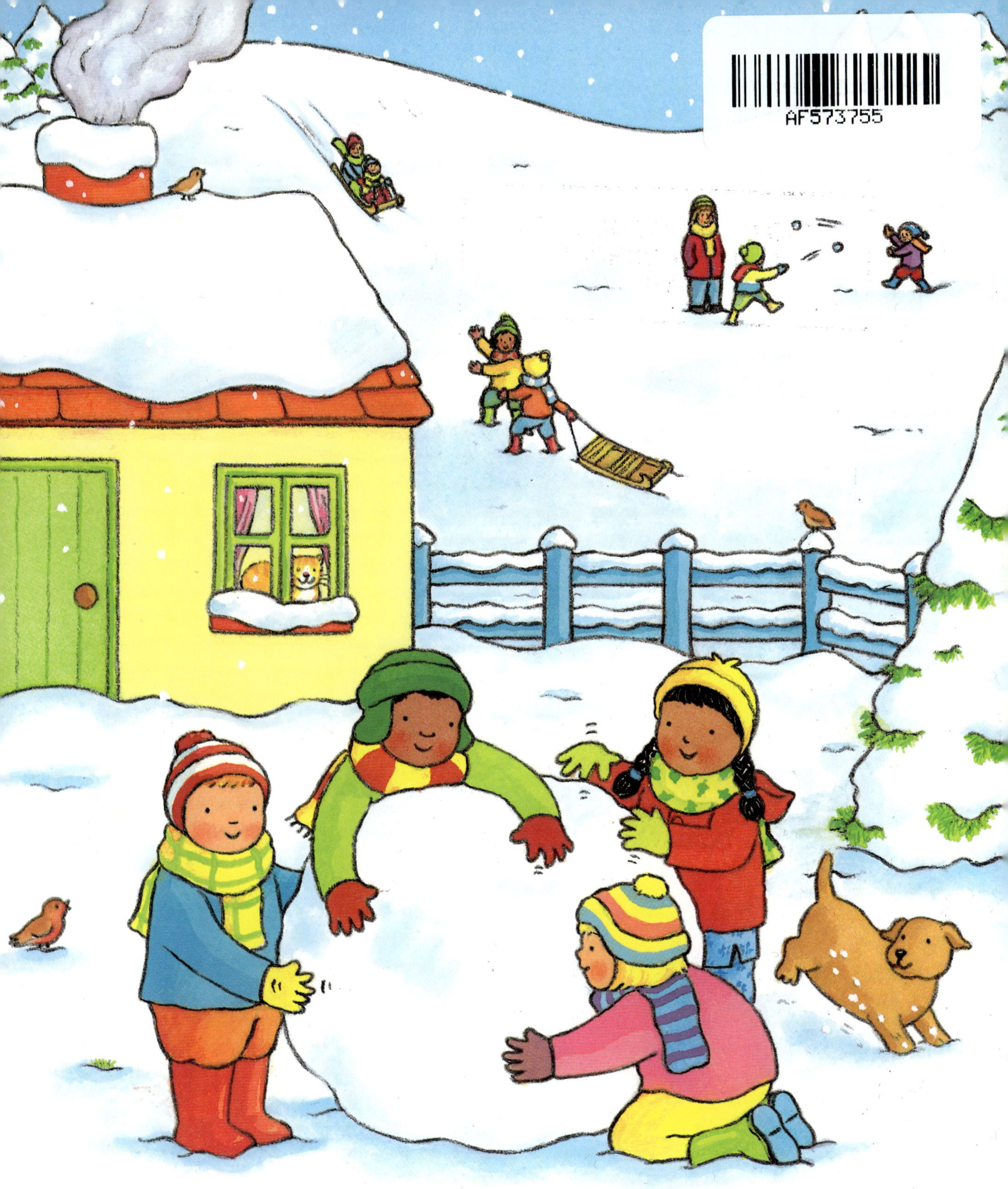

Pat the snow down, pat, pat, pat.

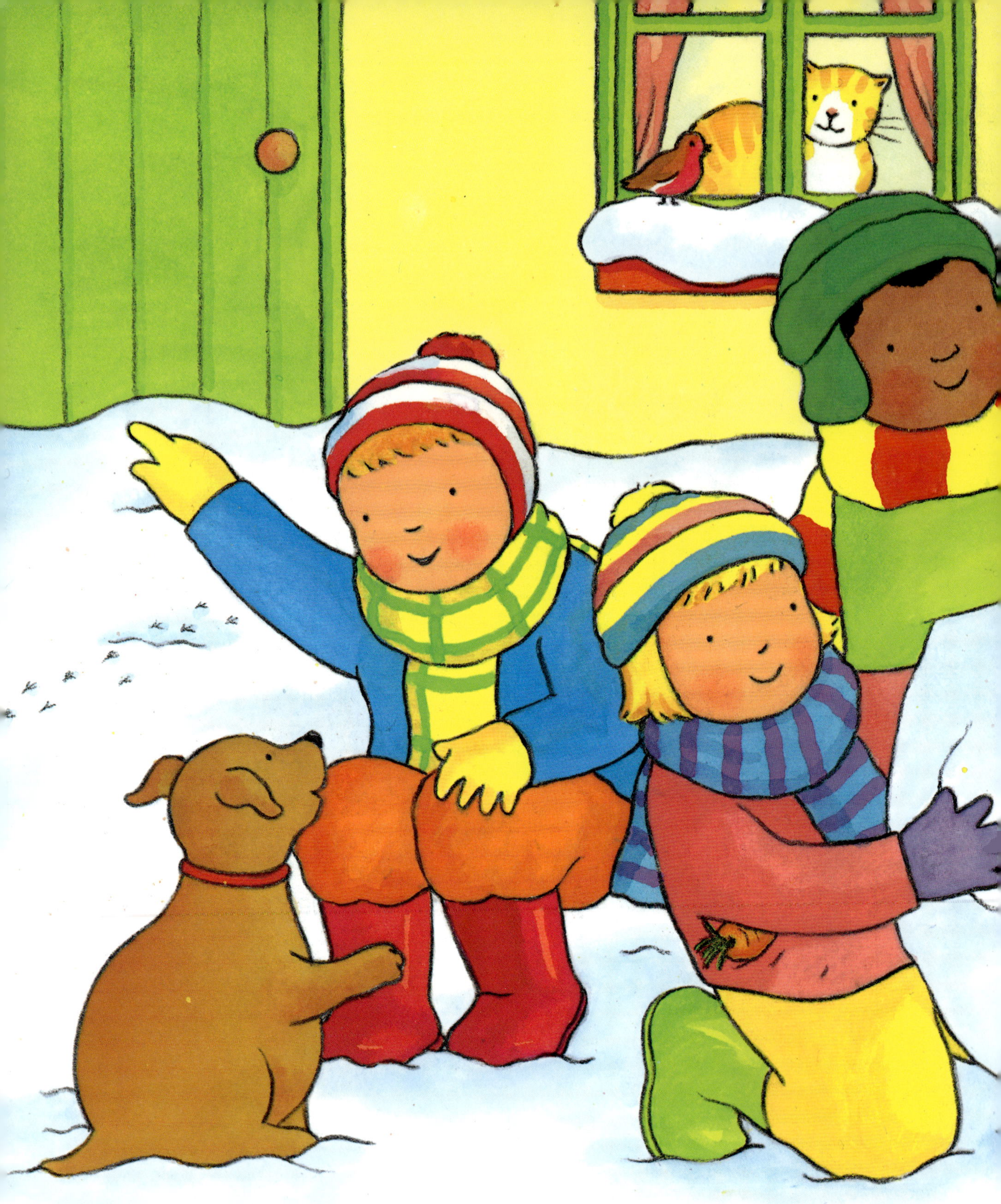

Make him big,

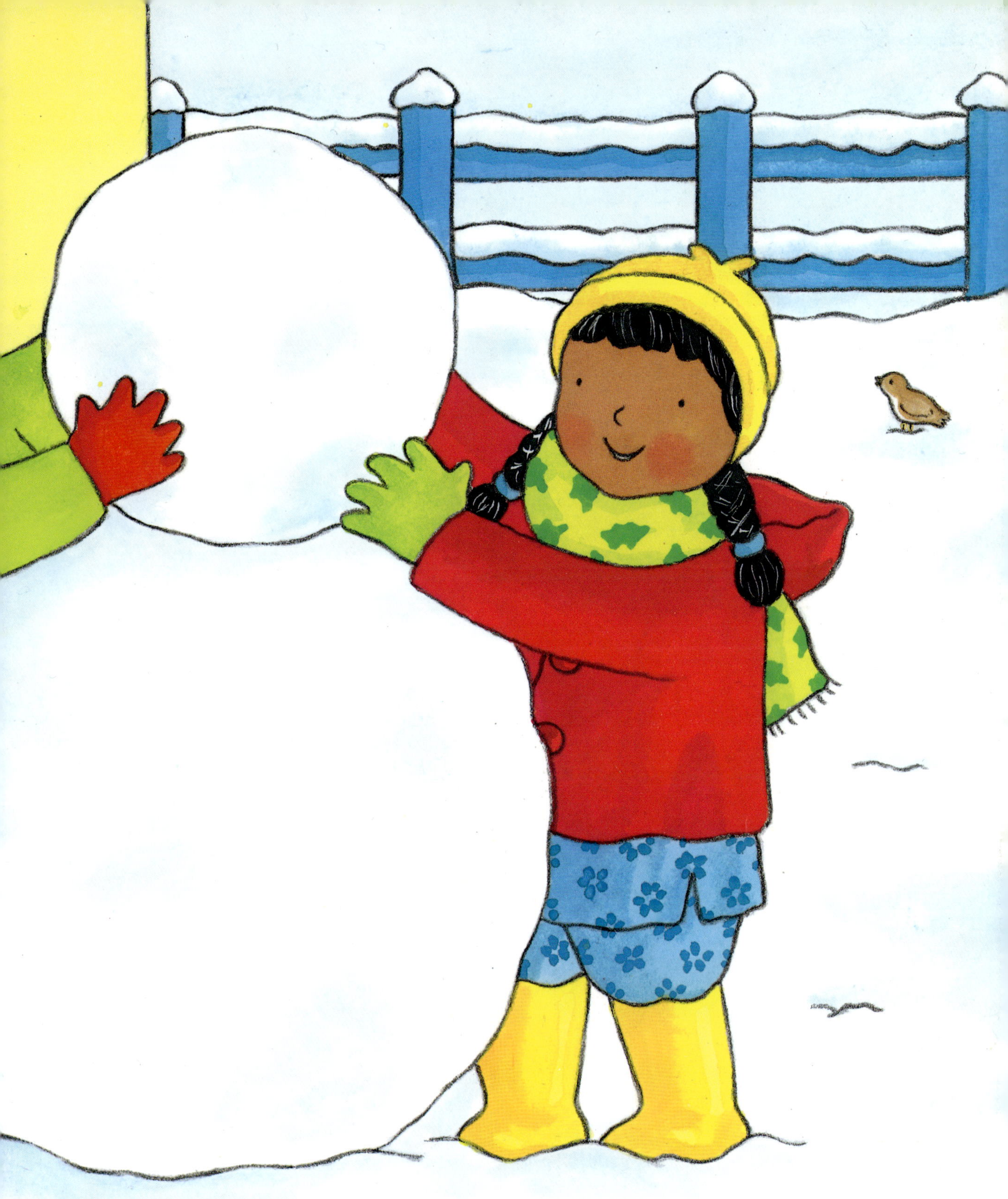

make him fat.

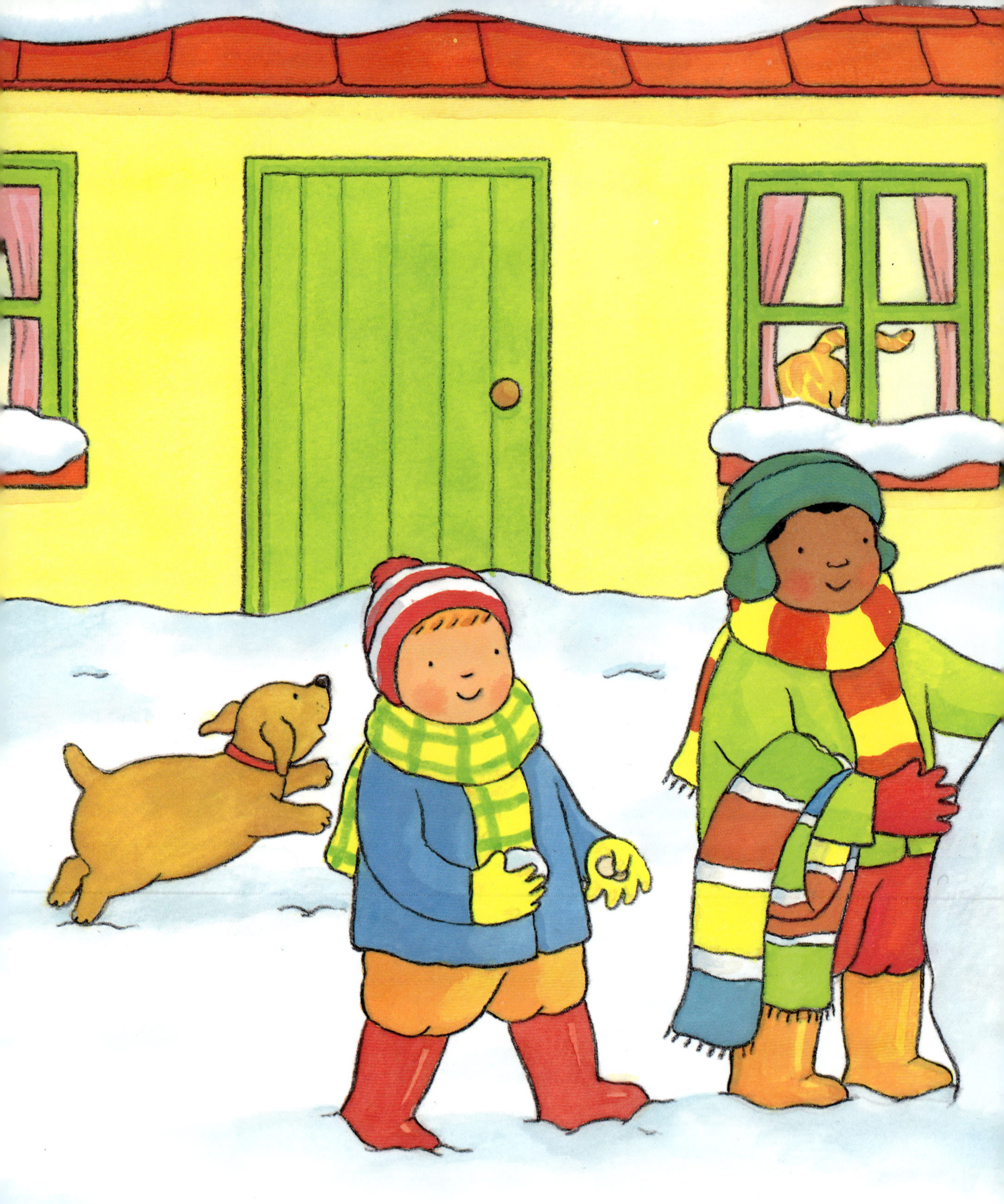

Pop on a nose,

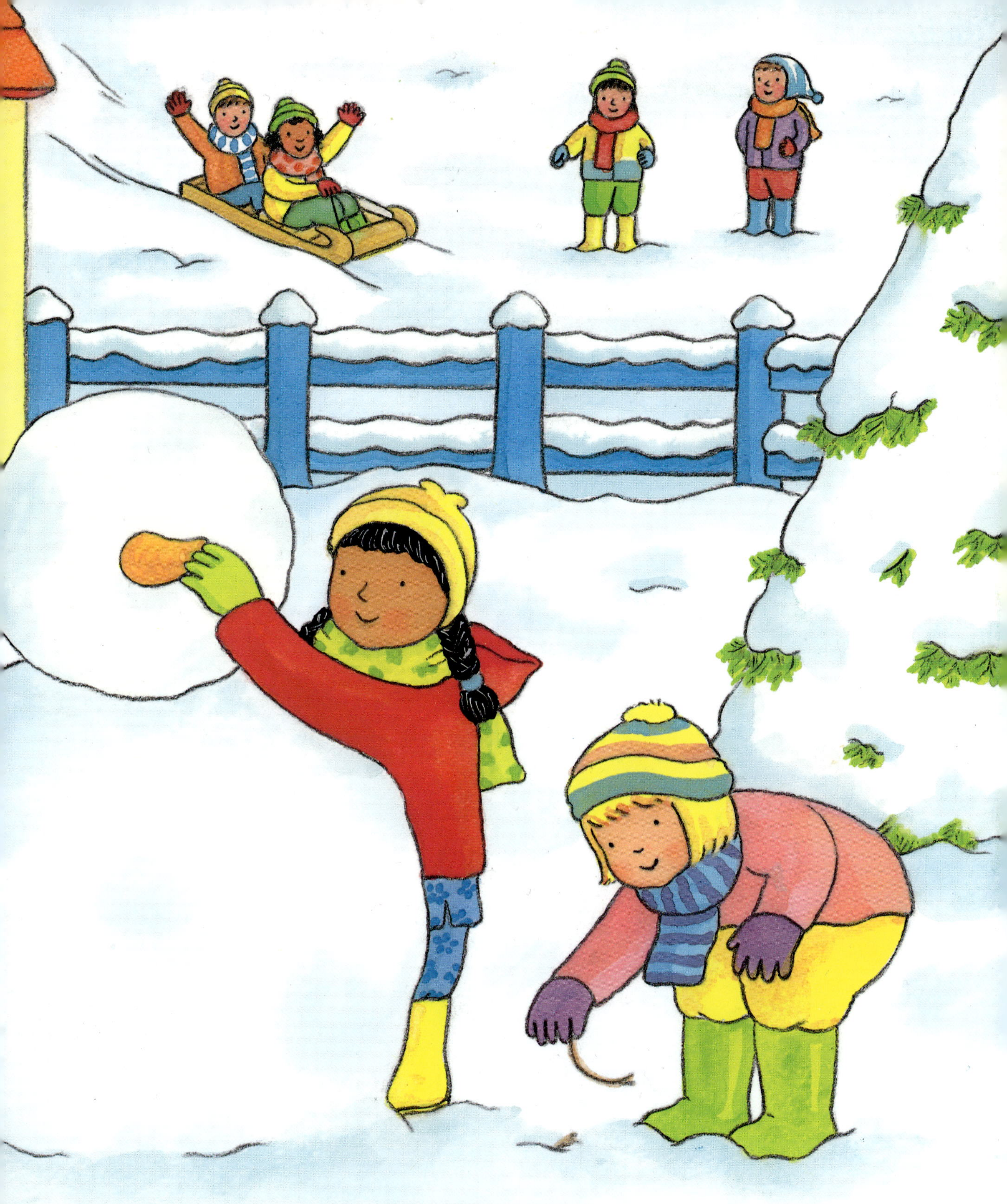

just like that.

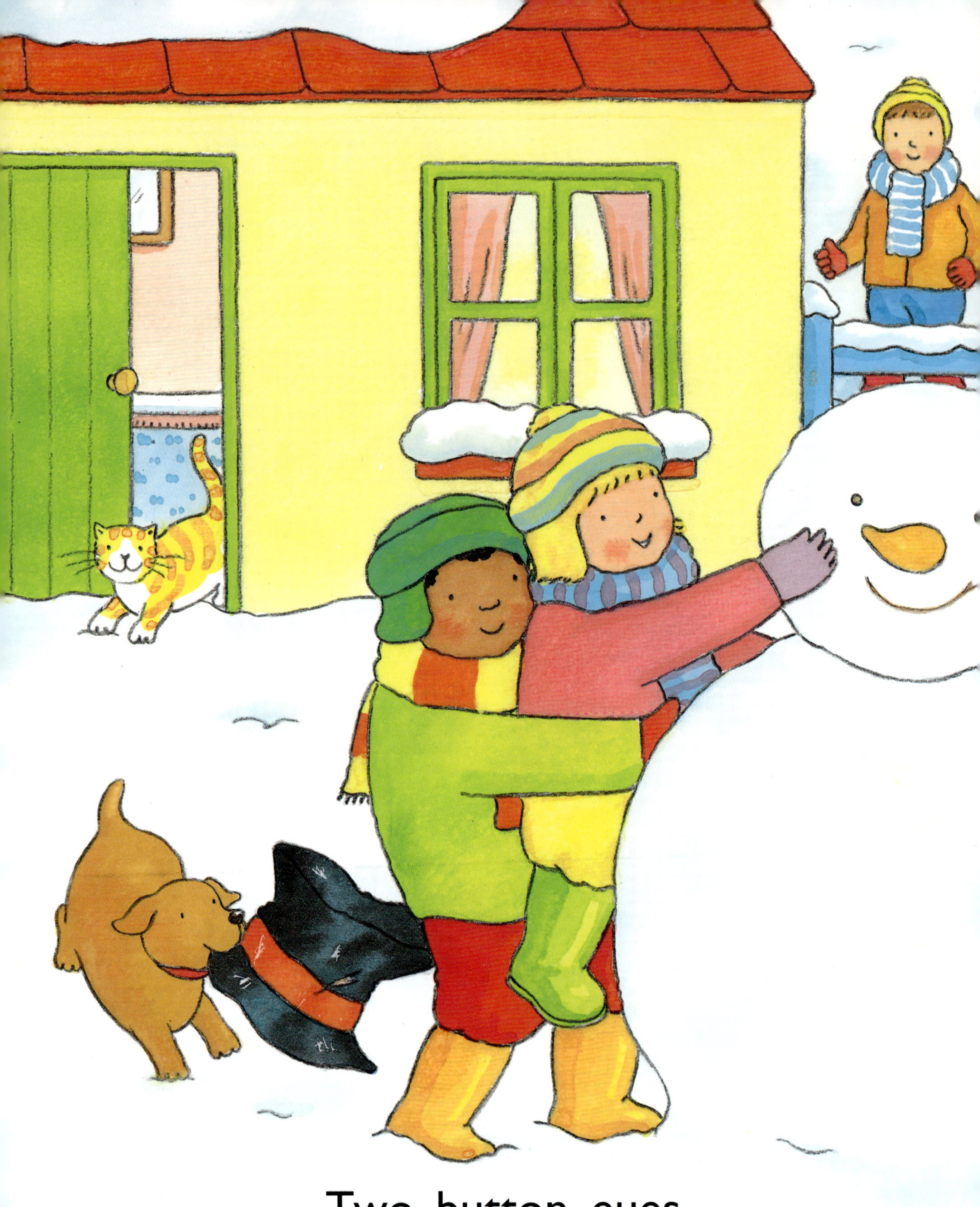

Two button eyes,

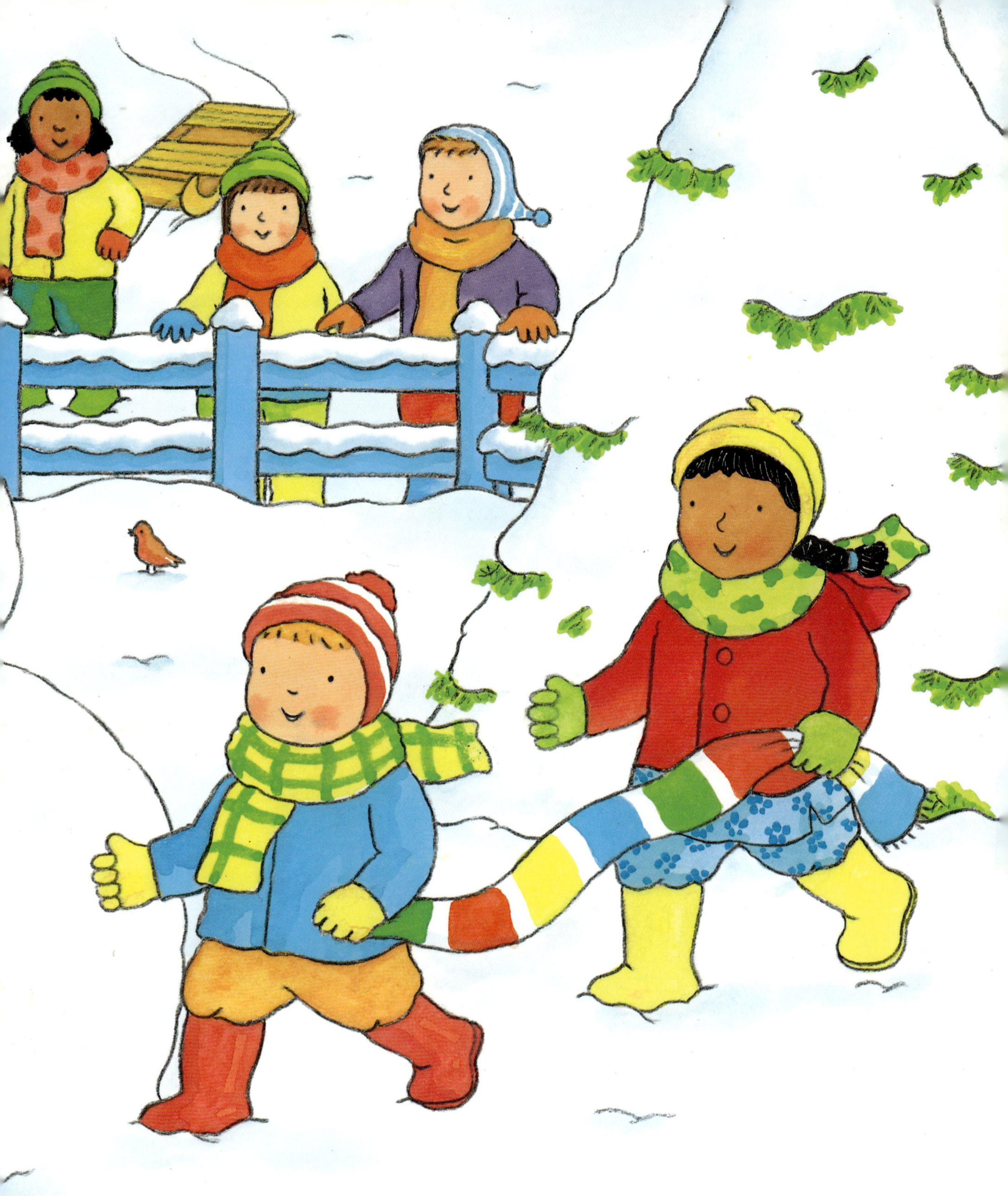

a grin like a cat.

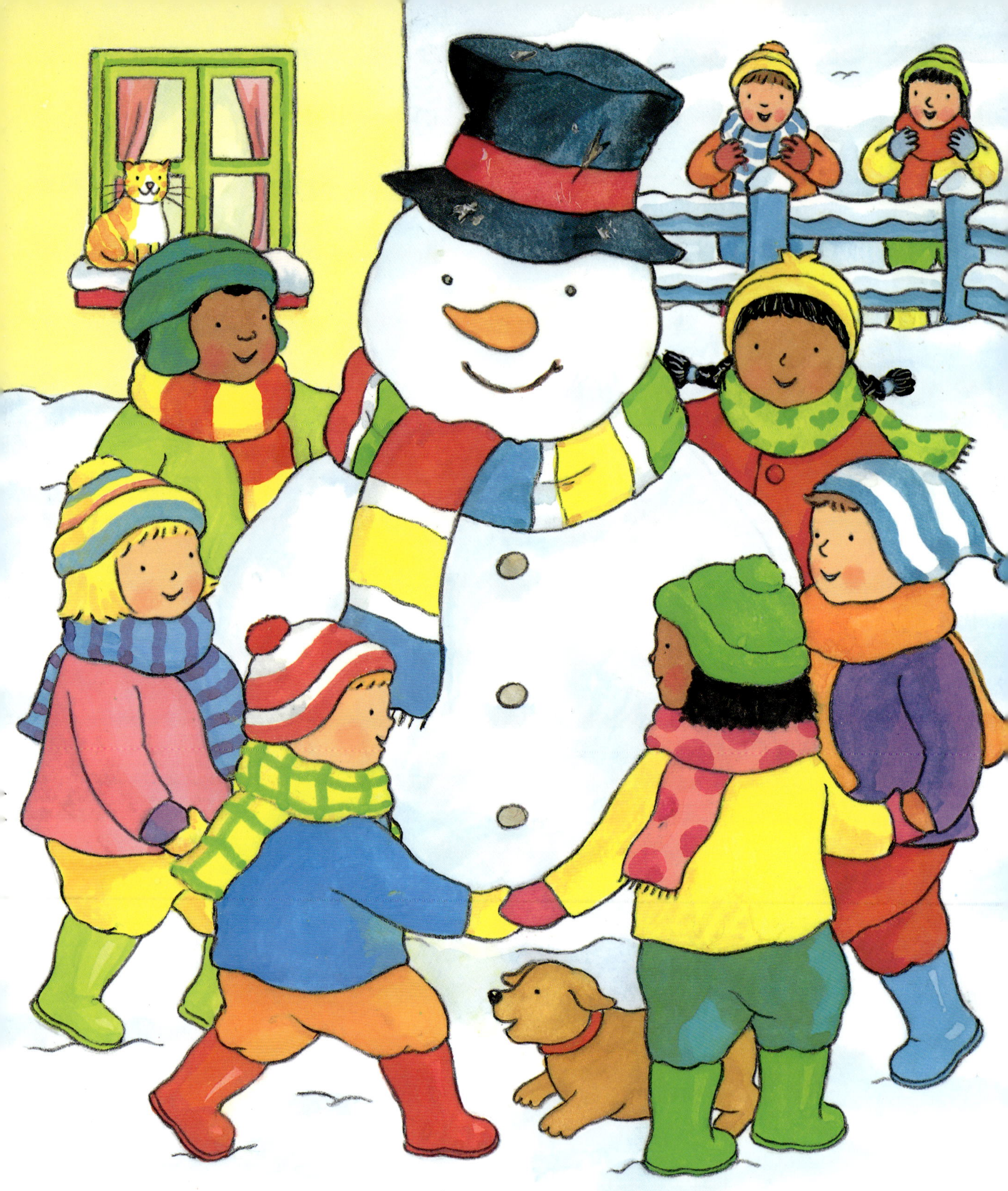

And on his head an old top hat.